Coming

HOME

Coming Home A Devotional Journal

Cover and Interior design by: Mark Ross / MJ Ross Design
Project Editor: Alice Sullivan
Devotions written by Rev. Èmile Hawkins, Sr. and Rev. Danny Lynchard in
association with ProvidenceWorks LLC.
Cover photo by Thinkstock ©2004

Photos shown with the letters are taken from the **Cornelius WWII Collection**
and are not those of the letter writer unless otherwise noted.

Coming
HOME

A Devotional Journal

ELM HILL BOOKS
A Division of Thomas Nelson Publishers
Since 1798

www.thomasnelson.com

This devotional is a wonderful tribute to all the men and women bravely serving our country. It is also special, though, because it reaches out not only to these incredible Soldiers, Marines, Airmen, and Sailors, but to the vast network of family and friends on the homefront waiting anxiously to be reunited with their loved ones. Their patience, their love, and their support are integral to our military's success, and they deserve the gratitude of our entire nation. And to these families and friends, I say God bless you for all that you do, and I hope all of your prayers are answered, and most important, that all of our troops return home safely.

— Andrew Carroll, director of the Legacy Project and editor of the national bestseller, *"WAR LETTERS: Extraordinary Correspondence from American Wars."*

Share copies of your letters or e-mails home with **Andrew Carroll**, director of the *Legacy Project*, which preserves wartime correspondences to honor and remember those who serve:

PO Box 53250
Washington, DC 20009
www.warletters.com

Introduction

Around the world, men and women are sacrificing their time and lives in the pursuit of freedom. Wherever they are, whatever their circumstances might be, families and friends must sacrifice with them. *Coming Home, A Devotional Journal,* is designed to give comfort, wisdom, guidance and strength while encouraging and supporting the efforts of those who serve and those who wait.

Read and see the emotion of original letters from previous wars. Hear and feel the cadences used daily by military personnel worldwide. Believe and trust that your prayers can help bring peace throughout the world and return all people safely home.

As you record your thoughts and prayers in this journal, may you know that God is sovereign over all life; His strength will become your strength, and trust that He is in control over all things.

"Father, if it is Your will, take this cup away from Me; nevertheless not My will, but Yours, be done." Luke 22:42

Packing for Peace

*Grace to you and peace from God our Father
and the Lord Jesus Christ.*

I Corinthians 1:3

His parents' bed was so high, the little boy had to place his
hands on the edge and peer over to watch his father pack
for deployment. As the young soldier grabbed the last
item, the wide-eyed little guy arched his eyebrows and
said, "Dad, are you packing for war?" Tossing the Bible in
his case, his father answered,

"No son, daddy's packing for peace."

Meek yet Mighty

"…be strong in the Lord and in the power of His might."

Ephesians 6:10

When we do what is right, even when it feels wrong, we become the only thing that stands between freedom and anarchy. Do what is right, season it with mercy, and let God work all things for good.

Lord, give me the vision to know what is right. And even more importantly, give me the strength to do it.

My Personal Partner

O wretched man that I am! Who will deliver me from this body of death? I thank God—through Jesus Christ our Lord!

Romans 7:24, 25

Many talk of God saving us from sin. Not enough talk of how He can save us from ourselves.

Lord, walk into my battlefield with me, whether it be filled with enemies that know me not, or with personal struggles that know me all too well.

Therefore be merciful, just as your Father also is merciful.

Luke 6:36

What a conflict the word mercy has with the word war! Yet, there are occasions when war can be motivated by the desire for mercy to the oppressed—to silence hate, to protect the innocent. The nobility of war is not found in planning rooms, political parties, or lecture halls, but in the soul of the soldier who has determined in his heart to perform an act of mercy.

Father, judge my heart and make it one of mandatory mercy.

Small Things—Great Value

And those members of the body which we think to be less honorable, on these we bestow greater honor…

I Corinthians 12:23

The greatness of a country is not always defined by the grandeur of its buildings, the wealth of its economy, or extent of its opportunities for advancement. Sometimes greatness is found in those small and simple acts of love repeated and multiplied until they become the very fabric of a nation.

Lord, help me realize that everything I do for You and for others becomes an act of love for all.

World War I

"I keep thinking what a different world it will be to mothers; when you all come marching home again! And when you do come marching home old fellow bring me back the same boy I gave my country,—true, and clean, and gentle, and brave.

–Mother"

*Written by **Kate Gordon** in a letter to one of her three sons who were serving in WWI. Jimmy, age eighteen and the youngest of the three boys, would be killed in the war. John and Luke would return home to the States in 1919.*

Giving Up To Gain

"...not My will, but Yours, be done."

Luke 22:42

Not only is this a statement of submission, but of wisdom. For in that one statement we place our hopes, dreams, plans, and projects into the hands of a God who wants to bless us more than we want to bless ourselves. We want answers that seem to be best for the now. God wants answers that are best for our tomorrows, and only He knows what our tomorrows hold.

Father, into Thy hands do I commit my life's path and problems.

Keep your heart with all diligence, For out of it spring the issues of life.

Proverbs 4:23

The calling of God is deeper than a call to specific tasks. It is a call to a specific meaning and purpose. It is revealed in the way we interpret our duty.

Lord, I want to be Your instrument of help to the hurting I see today. I ask You to help me serve from my heart, for it is there Your greatest wisdom is revealed. It is there Your greatest love can be understood and it is there You live and visit me.

Determined Hope

> *I would have lost heart, unless I had believed That I would see the goodness of the Lord In the land of the living.*

Psalms 27:13

These words were spoken in the same part of the world our soldiers find themselves today. It was a world of hot blowing sand, filled with an enemy longing for their demise. Yet this man's faith in a God who would bring him home gave him strength.

Lord, use my letters, words, and prayers to give our young men and women strength to know they will come home safe and victorious.

The Sanctity Of Serving

And Jesus answered…, "Martha, Martha, you are worried and troubled about many things. But one thing is needed, and Mary has chosen that good part…"

Luke 10:41, 42

"Women" and "war" are words that are difficult to reconcile. Yet women also are called to serve. When Mary served at the feet of Jesus, and Martha needed her to serve in the kitchen, Jesus responded, "Mary has chosen that which is needful." Both were serving in different ways.

Sometimes active duty means, "Love in action"—with a capital "L."

15

World War II

"We of the United States have something to fight for—
never more fully have I realized that. There is no other
country with comparable wealth, advancement, or
standard of living. The U.S.A. is worth a sacrifice!"

*2nd Lt. Jack Lundberg was the lead navigator on a B-17 flying over
Abbeville, France. He died in antiaircraft fire and was buried in the
American Cemetery in Normandy, France alongside his comrades.*

In His Grip!

For I, the Lord your God, will hold your right hand,
Saying to you, 'Fear not, I will help you.'

Isaiah 41:13

When God says He will hold your hand, please don't mistake it for a hand-patting comfort session. He is about to infuse you with His strength, His might, and His fight! You will find God to be the soldier's Soldier. He watches your back while putting your life on track. With God's help, you will find the ability to do the impossible.

Precious Lord, take my hand.

DATE

It Starts In The Heart

*"...What man is there who is fearful and fainthearted?
Let him go and return to his house, lest the heart of his
brethren faint like his heart."*

Deuteronomy 20:8

Faintheartedness is much greater than simple fear. Rather
than work through the fear, faintheartedness empowers
fear to govern our actions. It is full of words like "can't"
and "impossible." And worst of all, it is contagious! It
infects our actions and conversations. We serve a God who
makes the impossible possible—and He has chosen to do
it first in the hearts of people.

*Let's open our hearts to God's Spirit and close it to lesser
things like fear and doubt.*

18

Deploying Faith

You shall not be afraid of the terror by night, Nor of the arrow that flies by day, Nor of the pestilence that walks in darkness, Nor of the destruction that lays waste at noonday.

Psalms 91:5, 6

Nothing in life can keep us from needing to depend on the goodness and grace of God.

Father, help me know that I must be trained to trust You more than I trust my equipment.

A Standing Shield

*I will camp around My house Because of the army,
Because of him who passes by and him who returns.
No more shall an oppressor pass through them, For
now I have seen with My eyes.*

Zechariah 9:8

Lord, You are my Guard and my Shield. Sometimes You
place me to represent You as a guard against things that
hurt. Help me to see through the eyes of faith that You
are with me.

*Help me to remain strong and steadfast so that others
are safe behind me.*

The backslider in heart will be filled with his own ways, But a good man will be satisfied from above.

Proverbs 14:14

Life is full of surprises. It can also be full of expectancies and planned outcomes. The life that God wants for us is a life full of His presence and sure rewards. Although we may wonder why others seem to get away with wrong actions, God will deal with them in His own way.

Rewards come for doing the right thing.

DATE

Launched From The Peak

He shall cover you with His feathers, and under His wings you shall take refuge; His truth shall be your shield and buckler.

Psalms 91:4

The most frightening moment in the life of a young eagle is the time he is forced from his lofty perch into the mountain air. His greatest comfort is in knowing he was designed for such a purpose, and a greater eagle is there to support him. Soldiers must believe God has prepared them and that their country is behind them. Then, they too can fly.

Lord, show me the wisdom of Your ways and the support of Your people.

World War II

"When I get enough money to buy a new car and a house I'll come back and we'll get married. You wouldn't like California though because they have cockroaches out here bigger than my car."

Sgt. Don Gore to his girlfriend who lived in a different state.

An Outreaching Reach

Then He will answer them, saying, 'Assuredly, I say to you, inasmuch as you did not do it to one of the least of these, you did not do it to Me.'

Matthew 25:45

The caring hands of God may often be at the end of a uni-formed sleeve. Through you, He can bring the hands of the greatest Healer to the greatest hurt.

Lord, I may see some of the most hurt people in the world. Let my hands become an extension of Your own as I reach out to help.

My Secret Place

DATE

You are my hiding place; You shall preserve me from trouble; You shall surround me with songs of deliverance.

Psalms 32:7

When we were children, most of us had a hiding place. A place where we felt that no one could find us unless we wanted them to. We read our books there, played with our toys, and sometimes invited a friend (as long as they swore not to tell). We could stay there for hours on end. With the Lord, we also have a hiding place. A place where we are surrounded by His love and presence.

Think of the Lord as your hiding place!

25

Divine Design

> *For I know the thoughts that I think toward you, says the Lord, thoughts of peace and not of evil, to give you a future and a hope.*

> Jeremiah 29:11

God is strategic in His plans. We must follow His lead in making plans for the future. Once you have reached the end of your planning, you must then rewind the tape to the beginning with the end in mind, and start living your life by a divine design. God will strengthen your resolve. He will correct any plans you have made in error. Your vision of the future is not the problem, your strategy is.

Submit your plan to God and He will adjust it accordingly.

On The Right Side

For I, the Lord your God, will hold your right hand,
Saying to you, 'Fear not, I will help you.'

Isaiah 41:13

In Hebrew culture, the right hand is the hand of strength, authority, and power. When God upholds you with His right hand, He not only strengthens you, He gives you the strength to conquer all of your fears. Through your faith, you have His delegated authority to declare that mountains be removed. You have His authority!

Know that there is nothing on earth mightier than the Word of God.

Dec. 25, 1864
I wish you all a merry Christmas
Savannah, GA

Once more under the protecting hand of God and the waving of the American flag I am permitted to address a few lines to my beloved parents.

We left Atlanta on the 15th day of November and arrived in Savannah on the 21st of this month during which time we have been without mail or communications from any source. We marched over 300 miles right through the heart of Georgia and tore up the R.R. all the way from Atlanta to this place…I stood the march well, walked all the way and carried my knapsack. We ran out of rations before we got through and everyone had to look out for himself for more than two weeks, we lived on sweet potatoes and beef. My shoes gave out and I have been barefoot for three weeks and a good many others are in the fix, but the weather is very warm and we don't suffer with cold any…

I am looking anxiously for a letter from you every day, perhaps one will come today. You must write soon, give my love to all…We did not hear [how] the election went until we got here. I tell you there was some cheering when we heard that Abe was elected.

I must close. Yours as ever,
C. H. Lewis

*Letter written from **C.H. Lewis** to his parents during the Civil War.*

Lift Your Thoughts Aloft

"For as the heavens are higher than the earth, So are My ways higher than your ways, And My thoughts than your thoughts."

Isaiah 55:9

He or she who thinks traditionally can only rise to levels already reached.

Lord, there are many ways I can be Your servant and do my duty. Lift my thinking until I think the thoughts of God—until I see with Your eyes and serve as Your hands.

Sometimes No Answer

For in You, O Lord, I hope; You will hear,
O Lord my God.

Psalms 38:15

In prayer, we make our requests known to the Lord. In many
instances, His answer is not apparent. Being involved in
difficult circumstances, such as a deployment, often causes
one to pray prayers with great expectation and anticipation.
Trust that God hears you. And remember, sometimes no
answer IS His answer.

The Selected Ones

*Moreover you shall select from all the people able men,
such as fear God, men of truth, hating covetousness;
and place such over them to be rulers of thousands,
rulers of hundreds, rulers of fifties, and rulers of tens.*

Exodus 18:21

No war has ever been won by the efforts of a man or woman
operating alone. It takes capable men and women selected
for their skills, discipline, fortitude, and "espirt de corps."
Be encouraged! You are a part of God's strategic plan.

A Weapon Of Warfare

But immediately He talked with them and said to them, "Be of good cheer! It is I; do not be afraid."

Mark 6:50

Perhaps one of the greatest elements that defeats us a thousand times more than a weapon of warfare, is fear. There is no greater assurance, no greater resolve, than for the words of Jesus to reverberate in our hearts and minds—

—*"don't be afraid!"*

The Real You

Then David said to the Philistine, "You come to me with a sword, with a spear, and with a javelin. But I come to you in the name of the Lord of hosts, the God of the armies of Israel, whom you have defied."

I Samuel 17:45

They train you and train you but nothing compares to the real life conflict. Who you are comes out. Battle training is about building reflexes and decision-making ability. It is about what you are not who you are. The "who" is built by parents, friends, life conflicts, and a relationship with the Lord. Surround yourself with those who make you proud of who you are as well as what you are.

Lord, draw me close to You so I may be more like You.

33

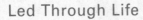

Led Through Life

> *"I will bring the blind by a way they did not know; I will lead them in paths they have not known. I will make darkness light before them, and crooked places straight. These things I will do for them, and not forsake them."*

Isaiah 42:16

"Life is not an easy matter...You cannot live through it without falling into frustration and cynicism unless you have before you a great idea that raises you above personal misery, above weakness, above all kinds of perfidy and baseness." *[Leon Trotsky] Diary In Exile, Entry for April 3, 1935*

Lord, give me new, creative, and safe ways to do my tasks. You place in my hands the power to deal with people, the good, the bad, and the troubled. May Your wisdom teach me how to deal with each one.

September 20, 1918

Dearest Woman,

Finished your letter last evening, but had to cut it short, as we moved into a new area last night. My girl, my girl, how I do miss you. I didn't think it possible for one to be possessed of the longing I have for you. At night I lay awake and think and think of you, the roar of the big guns, giving way before the press of mental pictures of you. I go back and re-travel again the entire road that we have known together…

If I had to go over the same road with you again, I am quite sure the way would be easier for you. The mistakes I have made, the heartaches I have caused you stand out like the shell holes that deface much of this country that once was so beautiful. I am learning my lesson, honey, and this experience, this absence from you, is burning its brand into my soul as nothing has ever done before.

Must break off again. Will continue tomorrow. Good night and God bless and preserve you.

Write—write.

2nd Lt. Francis M. Tracy, September 20, 1918, to his wife Gertrude during WWI. They fell in love and were married when she was only eighteen. They were together for eleven years before Tracy was shipped off to France and he frequently wrote while serving in the Ninety-first Division. He was killed September 27, 1918.

The Nature Of A Name

I will give you the treasures of darkness And hidden riches of secret places, That you may know that I, the Lord, Who call you by your name, Am the God of Israel.

Isaiah 45:3

Our name is the most personal thing we own. Those syllables contain our past, our present, and our future. To be called by your name is to be recognized as a unique person, not just one of a multitude.

That is how God wants to know you… and you to know Him.

Run "To"—Not "From"

DATE

…when you run, you will not stumble.

Proverbs 4:12

When the Bible speaks of the command to run, it is always in reference to a charge, not a retreat. It is a great lesson in life never to be found running "from" but running "to." Soldiers of God are not found to run from evil, but to defeat evil by running to God.

Lord, guide my steps so that I may run focused on the goal and not my feet.

Right Regardless of Retribution

*He who follows righteousness and mercy Finds life,
righteousness and honor.*

Proverbs 21:21

Doing right is no guarantee against misfortune. It can,
however, guarantee the satisfaction of having done the
very best you could.

*Lord, when I have done my best, and yet failed at success,
help me place the result in Your hands and rise to try again.*

...that they all may be one, as You, Father, are in Me, and I in You; that they also may be one in Us, that the world may believe that You sent Me.

John 17:21

The call to service must always be greater than the servant. The nobility of the task should never be diminished by the smallness of a prideful attitude.

Lord, let my calling be more important than my worries and personal gain. May I always see that true gain comes by Your hand and not by the accolades of comrades.

April 22, 1918, WWI

Dear Charlie and Teddy:

I have received several very nice letters from you both. What a time you did have with the measles, did you not? Well the time to have them is when you are young so you will not catch them when you get older…

How do you like the picture of your dad, dug out, and the little accelerator behind him? One thing over here, the more rank one has the better dug out, sometimes that makes me wish I were president.

Now I must close but I want you both to do something for me. Go to mother, put both your arms around her neck and give her a kiss for dad and tell her that although dad scolds her sometimes in his letters and is pretty much of an old grouch, he loves her with all his heart. Now boys be good and take care of the only girl in our family.

Dad.

Maj. Edward B. Cole to his two young sons.

When Sacrifice Becomes Sweet

And walk in love, as Christ also has loved us and given Himself for us, an offering and a sacrifice to God for a sweet-smelling aroma.

Ephesians 5:2

Sacrifice is never so sweet as when it is made on behalf of someone else.

Father, help me remember the simple joy in giving the simple things in life. For the greater reward comes from the giving of a lot of small things over and over.

Surrender The Sword

"…Vengeance is Mine, I will repay," says the Lord.

Romans 12:19

The heart cry of every victim is for true justice. However, anger, retaliation, and revenge are sacrifices we must lay at the altar. Hanging onto the sword of reprisal risks losing the battle, and even worse, places us in the position of doing what only God has the wisdom to accomplish. Give the sword to God.

Lord, when I take up the sword, may it be at Your direction, not at my discretion.

Direction Even In Darkness

*If I say, "Surely the darkness shall fall on me,"
Even the night shall be light about me...*

Psalms 139:11

Early in the war with Afghanistan and Iraq, one of the F16 pilots was asked about the difficulty of night fighting. His response was, "It is the best time, for I own the night." He, of course, was referring to the state-of-the-art night vision equipment at his disposal. Yet, in a world sometimes darkened by evil, we can still see the good.

Lord, let me not be afraid of the night that surrounds me, for You own the night.

43

Help Will Come

"And whatever things you ask in prayer, believing, you will receive."

Matthew 21:22

In times of conflict, whether on the battlefront or on the home-front, ask God for help and know that it will come. From the insignificant situation to the extreme life-threatening situation, know that He hears you.

Stay prayerful. Stay connected to God and His Word.

A Powerful Shield

After these things the word of the Lord came to Abram
in a vision, saying, "Do not be afraid, Abram. I am your
shield, your exceedingly great reward."

Genesis 15:1

Often when the Lord speaks to us, He does so while we are surrounded by overwhelming circumstances. Yet if we listen to His voice, He stays near. God's shield is big and powerful enough to preserve us—and all who are with us. When we look to Him, He never fails.

His presence is our shield.

Forward Without Fear

In God (I will praise His word), In God I have put my trust; I will not fear. What can flesh do to me?

Psalms 56:4

Fear can defeat a man or an army before the first shot is fired. Don't let fear hinder you from making forward progress.

God will provide a strategy to conquer the enemy, even the enemy of fear.

July 29, 1944

Dearest Mae,

I promised you I'd write every chance I had so here I am again. In the lull, between firing, I've found that scribbling off a few lines of a letter was the best way to ease the tension of fighting. Any little thing we do to divert my mind and keep us busy when the fighting comes to a temporary halt, relaxes the nerves and rests our bodies.

That's why receiving mail from home is so important. I've got a bunch of letters in my pocket that are dirty and falling apart. They are the letters I have received from you, and the rest of the family. I almost know each one, word for word, 'cause I've read and re-read them so often. They are the ones that have kept me going until new ones come… I couldn't begin to tell you how much each letter from home means to me.

I know now, for certain, what we are fighting for! Our mission is to free all the nations of oppression. Give the children of this, and the coming generations a chance to grow decently, and learn the true meaning of the "Four Freedoms"… lots of love.

Ernest

Pfc. Ernest Uno, in a letter from Italy to his sister during WWII. Uno was with the famed Japanese-American 442nd Regimental Combat Team. He survived the war and returned to the United States, where he finished his schooling. After a thirty-year career with the YMCA, Uno studied for the deaconate in the Episcopal Church and became a deacon.

Humility And Honor Are Brothers

A man's pride will bring him low, But the humble in spirit will retain honor.

Proverbs 29:23

It is not our position in life that helps or hinders us with God. It is the condition of our heart.

Lord, let me carry my authority tempered with mercy. Help me remember that this is God's land, too, and that You have entrusted the people that live here in my care. Do not let those I meet under negative circumstances change my concern for those You have given me.

His Strength, My Strength

"Your right hand, O Lord, has become glorious in power; Your right hand, O Lord, has dashed the enemy in pieces."

Exodus 15:6

When in a trying situation, perhaps being tasked to accomplish objectives beyond your capabilities, your Father is there, giving you the strength and intelligence you need. When the dust settles, you will see that it was God whose power and might pulled you through.

You can do nothing without His power, and with His power, you cannot fail.

Path Of Peace

So David prevailed over the Philistine with a sling and a stone, and struck the Philistine and killed him…

I Samuel 17:50

The fact that you are compelled to use force does not make you a person of violence. Only the one who seeks violence as a way of personal gain or an avenue for quick solution is determined to be violent.

Lord, keep my feet from following violence. Yet, should it cross my path, let me be strong in the power of Your might.

Brave Women

Now Deborah, a prophetess, the wife of Lapidoth,
was judging Israel at that time.

Judges 4:4

Many of the homecoming videos and pictures of the past have highlighted our brave and courageous men. Today, there are thousands of women in harm's way who will one day come home to face many of the same scenarios as their counterparts. Through adversity, we have learned that bravery has no gender.

Thank God for courageous women!

"Sunday was topped off by a social gathering of the remaining battalion officers… Lt. Gutman raised this question—'What will the people back home say to us when we return? Will they call us suckers? They did those who fought in 1918!'—A strange hush fell over the officer, as if that was the question that all had thought about—all had worried about—We all realized how little people at home can conceive of the suffering, hardships, loneliness, violence of war.

We talked of the new generations—the teenagers that would look at their war tired brothers and fathers and speak of us as we once spoke of the men of the last war.—It wasn't pleasant—We knew then why so few veterans speak of their experiences.—No, not because they weren't exciting, new, dangerous—but because the squirts, the snot-noses, the know-it-alls had driven their souls to the background.

The young fathers wondered whether their kids would slam the door and run to mother shouting, "There's a strange man outside!"

Enough said—I love you—endlessly.

Your Sid

2nd Lt. Sidney Diamond in a letter to his fiancé, Estelle, during WWII.

None Left Behind

"… Fear not, for I have redeemed you; I have called you by name; You are mine."

Isaiah 43:1

No war effort is complete unless plans are made to bring our brave and valiant men and women home. Just think, at one time, the evil one held all humanity captive, but Christ Jesus, our commander and chief, rescued all, leaving no one behind because we are His own.

For this reason, let your heart be encouraged and your strength renewed.

Pursuing Experience

...I have learned by experience that the Lord has blessed me for your sake.

Genesis 30:27

During the Vietnam War, the enemy could often be neither seen nor heard, except by those soldiers who had been there long enough to recognize the sights and sounds identifying his position. The proficiency of these soldiers kept others alive and came at the cost of experience. Experience comes of doing, sometimes by doing wrong, by failing, and by getting up stronger and wiser to do it again.

Lord, let me live each day as if it is practice for better tomorrows—for my comrades and myself.

When Patience Is An Option

I waited patiently for the Lord; And He inclined to me, And heard my cry. He also brought me up out of a horrible pit, Out of the miry clay, And set my feet upon a rock, And established my steps. He has put a new song in my mouth…

Psalms 40:1-3

One of the greatest gifts we have is the gift of patience. As a soldier, or one under another's authority, there is no question in the speedy execution of a command. In these cases, patience is not an option. A split second can make the difference between life or death, loss or victory.

I thank God that today patience will be an option—the ammunition for peace.

55

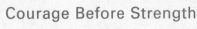

Courage Before Strength

Be of good courage, And He shall strengthen your heart,
All you who hope in the Lord.

Psalms 31:24

Courage is being afraid and doing it anyway. Any pilot on
their first solo flight knows exactly what that means. Read
that scripture again! God asks us to be of good courage
and *then* He strengthens our heart. The only prerequisite
is to hope in the Lord first. The most spiritual person is
not one who knows no fear, but one who does and moves
forward anyway.

Lord, here I come with fear and faith. Strengthen my heart.

The Promise Of Purpose

*Only fear the Lord, and serve Him in truth
with all your Heart; for consider what
great things He has done for you.*

I Samuel 12:24

Sometimes we don't need a change in jobs, just an insight into the good that our job accomplishes. Sometimes our purpose may change. That doesn't mean the new one isn't just as valid.

Lord, when my way grows tired and I cannot see the good I am accomplishing, show me Your purpose so that I may find new strength and new joy.

Foxhole Lessons

Have we not all one Father? Has not one God created us?
Why do we deal treacherously with one another By
profaning the covenant of the fathers?

Malachi 2:10

The greatness of a nation may often be seen by its acceptance and generosity to the weary traveler and compatriot,
regardless of his race. The voice of prejudice is often the
voice of reason shrouded in fear and lack of understanding. There are no racists in foxholes. Perhaps by seeing all
of life as a foxhole and all of us as one army, we may find
the greatest moments of our life.

Father, help me to find a battle bigger than my prejudice.

"Somewhere in the Philippines—In combat again—a lot to say but—A. very tired—B. very dirty—C. Busy, Busy as all hell—Been moving constantly—Excuse brevity—I love you—you make my foxhole warm and soft—sweetheart—your Sid."

2nd Lt. Sidney Diamond, *January 19, 1945, WWII*

Replace Misplaced Confidence

It is better to trust in the Lord Than to put confidence in man.

Psalms 118:8

Because man is imperfect, whatever he creates is marked by his imperfection. Whatever God creates is marked by His trustworthiness.

Lord, help me not be surprised at the inadequacies of man, nor forget Your faithfulness, for I can trust You.

For God is not the author of confusion but of peace…

I Samuel 12:24

A tremendous explosion occurs and pandemonium begins with people running to and fro, emergency workers are overwhelmed. There are hundreds of questions, and fewer answers. This is the scene of an attack. Yet, amazingly, the right things seem to get done.

In the middle of the mayhem there is something bigger than us at work. It is God's spirit directing and guiding. It is where the peace is. It is there you will find your rest.

Salute Sowing

"Therefore, whatever you want men to do to you, do also to them, for this is the Law and the Prophets."

Matthew 7:12

Every enlisted person is required to salute all officers, regardless of rank or branch of service. Yet the same regulation requires every officer to return every salute "in the same manner as presented." There is no greater illustration of sowing and reaping, giving and gaining, or "doing unto others" as the salute. It is the most powerful military tool for both showing and commanding respect.

Lord, help me give to others that respect which I would like to receive.

God's Permanent Presence

*"And the Lord, He is the one who goes before you.
He will be with you, He will not leave you nor
forsake you; do not fear nor be dismayed."*

Psalms 118:8

Hiding in a cave in the Middle East, David sought safety
from the horrific heat and from an enemy who found
beheading a statement of victory. I suppose one could
never feel more alone. It was there he realized that
there is no cave so deep that God is not deeper still.

Lord, help me feel Your presence to know I am never alone.

My Dear Daughter, Anna Mary,

Some day I shall be able to tell you the condition under which I write this letter to you. You arrived in this world while I was several thousand miles from your mother's side. There were many anxious moments then and since. This message comes to you from somewhere in England. I pray to God it will be given to you on or about your tenth birthday. I hope also to be present when that is done…

Also I pray that the efforts of your daddy and his buddies will not have been in vain. That you will always be permitted to enjoy the great freedoms for which this war is being fought. It is not pleasant, but knowing that our efforts are to be for the good of our children makes it worth the hardships.

I want you to know that God gave to you for a mother the finest woman of His creation. I pray that you will grow to be as fine a person as she. I ask that you follow her guidance and her teachings. I know how much you mean to her at the time I write this letter. Such a love can never be forgotten.

It is time that I close this short message to you… I place you now in the hands of God. May He care for you and love you. May He see fit that we shall see one another very soon and keep us together into eternity, ever as He gave us His Son to seal our salvation.

Your loving dad
Walter Schuette

Lt. Walter Schuette did make it home from WW II alive and was able to read his letter to Anna Mary on her tenth birthday.

Mighty In Battle

*Who is this King of glory? The Lord strong
and mighty, The Lord mighty in battle.*

Psalms 24:8

Many have asked themselves within, "How well do I know
the Lord?" Further, "What do I know about power and
grace?" Our answer should be an allegiant reminder; The
Lord is the King of Glory, Mighty in battle—to which one
might add, battles big or small,

He is Lord of all.

Mercy!

Blessed are the merciful, For they shall obtain mercy.

Matthew 5:7

Mercy is something we need and hope to be given on a daily basis. When we are merciful, we are conscious of the distressed and are often times compelled to assist. Rest assured that the Lord is always compelled to assist His creation.

Lord, have mercy upon us.

Joy Unspeakable

I will call upon the Lord, who is worthy to be praised;
So shall I be saved from my enemies.

II Samuel 22:4

Lord, should I die today, every word of thanks and adoration would fall short in describing the wonderful goodness You have bestowed upon my life here on earth. Yet, my desire is to live so that Your praise will continue to vibrate across these vocal chords so that others may hear of Your strength and goodness on my behalf.

Steady Spiritual Strength

*Where can I go from Your Spirit? Or where can I flee from
Your presence? If I ascend into heaven, You are there; If
I make my bed in hell, behold, You are there. If I take the
wings of the morning, And dwell in the uttermost parts
of the sea, Even there Your hand shall lead me, And Your
right hand shall hold me.*

Psalms 139:7-10

What a powerful assurance this is that the Divine Presence
is here right now, providing comfort, strength, and peace
to all who are in trouble. God's "right hand" is always
there for the bruised and battered with answers in a form
right for every situation. Nothing can separate us from the
love of God.

*Lord, help me know that Your love reaches the highest
mountain and flows in the lowest valleys.*

Endless Supply

The Lord is my light and my salvation; Whom shall I
fear? The Lord is the strength of my life;
Of whom shall I be afraid?

Psalms 27:1

The words "strength of my life" literally mean "the supplier of my life." What a wonderful thought that God, who is eternal, can supply us with eternal life! No wonder we need not fear those things which are temporal, for in Christ, we do go on.

Unexpected Faith

*When Jesus heard these things, He marveled at him,
and said… "I have not found such great faith,
not even in Israel!"*

Luke 7:9, 10

What a powerful statement! Of whom was Jesus speaking?
Surely it was one of the great theologians of the day. Wrong!
It was a soldier, a Roman soldier. A leader of one hundred
other soldiers. A Centurion. One seasoned and scarred by
the battlefields of life and war. You, too, can be a person of
faith. As you ask for God's strength and live a life of principle
and purpose, you, too, may merit such a statement.

"Our national anthem has a line which is appropriate to quote here: 'The land of the free and the home of the brave.' The two go hand in glove. If we are not brave, we soon will not be free. No nation, or person, ever achieved greatness, or even success, without courage.

The greater the heights of achievement, the greater the strength and resolution demanded. America is now the greatest human achievement in history,… and the length of the shadow which we cast into the future depends on how tall we stand now, just as it always has."

Lt. Col. Gerald W. Massy III in a letter to his daughter Lynn, from Vietnam, February 2, 1968. At that time, there were over 500,000 troops in Vietnam.

The Spiritual Shield

Every word of God is pure; He is a shield to those who put their trust in Him.

Proverbs 30:5

The difference between God and man cannot be seen any clearer than as revealed in these words. Where God chooses to shield humanity in His love, man has used his fellow man as human shields to protect his own purpose and plan. It is the difference between love and lust. Whom would you rather serve?

Father, surround me with Your presence, protect me by Your power, and shield me with Your strength.

Migrating Prayers

...But He blesses the home of the just.

Proverbs 3:33

Surrounded by sand and strangers, a soldier's mind often travels home where fond memories offer a nice break from the tension at hand. Those memories stir emotions too deep for words, and desires too difficult to fulfill from foreign soil. As God's child, the soldier can do something... even from a barracks—pray! Prayer works from a distance.

Ask God to help those at home until you can get back.

Forever Favored

Lord, by Your favor You have made my mountain stand strong…

Psalms 30:7

Shrapnel, debris, and bullets can take a life at the speed of sound. Yet, the greatest defense is not armored vehicles or bulletproof vests. Greater than all of these, and more, is God's favor: A favor that has been given to those who put their faith and confidence in a God who loves them enough to put His own Son in harm's way.

O Lord, thank You for the favor You have given me through the offering of Your Son.

Practice At Perfection

...those who by reason of use have their senses
exercised to discern both good and evil.

Hebrews 5:14

Just as the airplane turned on final approach, the engine
sputtered to a stop. The pilot quickly switched the fuel
tank selector and the engine purred to life. Pilots have a
saying, "Everyone gets two bags. One is empty, the other
full of luck. The trick is to fill the empty sack with
experience before your luck bag is empty."

Lord help me see that every exercise is to make me
better at what I do.

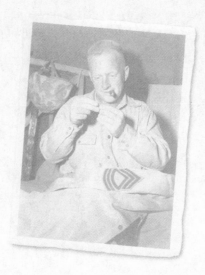

From Iraq

It means so much to receive a letter or package from someone we don't know that lets us know someone out there really appreciates the job we are doing over here... If it's not a problem, could you send us some Tang, Kool Aid, Oreos, Vienna sausages and Pringles?

May God bless you all,
SPC Keith Hunter

When you walk, your steps will not be hindered...

Proverbs 4:12

God places within the heart of His children an inner compass that always points them in His direction. When you walk in God's wisdom, no one can trip you up—and the road always leads home.

Lord, keep my footing sure, as my steps will eventually bring me home.

Rising From The Ashes Of War

Put on the whole armor of God, that you may be able to stand against the wiles of the devil.

Ephesians 6:11

How ironic that war would be a mechanism for peace, that injustice would engender justice, that the best in us arises in the worst of situations. To reveal evil in it's truest form requires the capacity to thwart it with the very thing it hates—Love. This is the only legitimate purpose of war. This is what Jesus did.

Lord, help me to see that true love must exist for the common good and therefore, must sometimes be tough.

Healing Relationships

Heal me, O Lord, and I shall be healed; Save me, and I shall be saved, For You are my praise.

Jeremiah 17:14

For some, distance and lengthy time away from loved ones causes disruptions within relationships. Although thankful for the numerous emails and phone calls, nothing takes the place of "being there." Often overlooked is the hurt and emptiness of separation. Do a relationship check, then ask the Lord to help.

Your relationship at home is only as good as Your relationship with God.

Flying By Faith

I will instruct you and teach you in the way you should go; I will guide you with My eye.

Psalms 32:8

As a new pilot, I flew into a frontal system only a few miles from my destination. With no instrument flight experience, I soon found myself feeling one thing while the instruments showed another. I began talking aloud, "Don't trust yourself. Look at your instruments." Within a mile of the airport, I broke through the lower layer of clouds right over my destination.

The Bible is your instrument panel. Trust it and it will take you home.

Now the Lord had said to Abram: "Get out of your country, From your family And from your father' house, To a land that I will show you."

Genesis 12:1

Leaving for war can be arduous to say the least. However, coming home to those who do not respect a soldier's valiant efforts can be just as confusing. In both, we need the Lord's guidance to show us not only how to survive, but how to thrive.

God will guide us with His voice.

No Guarantees

You will keep him in perfect peace, Whose mind is stayed on You, Because he trusts in You.

Isaiah 26:3

Can war ever guarantee peace? No! However, like the many wars around the world, personal conflicts can be numerous. Leaving war-torn countries after peace has been established gives us hope that at home, perpetual peace will also exist if we look to the Lord for help.

Peace is worth fighting for!

November 18, 1989
Dear Sir,

For twenty-two years I have carried your picture in my wallet. I was only eighteen years old that day that we faced one another on that trail in Chu Lai, Vietnam. Why you did not take my life I'll never know. You stared at me for so long armed with your AK-47 and yet you did not fire. Forgive me for taking your life, I was reacting just the way I was trained…

So many times over the years I have stared at your picture and your daughter, I suspect. Each time my heart and guts would burn with the pain of guilt. I have two daughters myself now.

As of today we are no longer enemies. I perceive you as a brave soldier defending your homeland… I'll sign off now Sir, so until we chance to meet again in another time and place, rest in peace.

Respectfully,
Richard A. Luttrell
101ˢᵗ Airborne Div.

Richard A Luttrell in a letter left at the Vietnam Memorial Wall in Washington DC. In March 2000, Luttrell located the daughter of the slain Vietnamese soldier in a village in Vietnam and returned this photograph he had kept. They cried in each other's arms.

"Offerings at the Wall: Artifacts from the Vietnam Veterans, Memorial Collection" (Turner Publishing, 1995; Atlanta, GA)

What To Do ...

Your word is a lamp to my feet And a light to my path.

Psalms 119:105

Having the wisdom and the ability to be a good husband or wife, as well as to raise children, takes something beyond us. It takes God. For those considering re-enlisting and making a career of the military, the Lord's wisdom is required. Every area of our lives, no matter the extent, requires the Lord's leading in order for us to be successful.

Let Jesus be the light of your life!

DATE

With gladness and rejoicing they shall be brought;
They shall enter the King's palace.

Psalms 45:15

Sitting on a plane headed for home, Clint's mind traveled forward only a few hours, preparing himself for his homecoming. His heart beat faster as his mind's eye drew pictures of his mom, his dad, and his girlfriend, all waiting to meet him. He knew their question would eventually be, "How was Iraq?" He settled on four words... hot, dangerous, frightening, and fun.

Lord, fill our hearts with rejoicing every day.

Home To Rest

Therefore my heart is glad, and my glory rejoices;
My flesh also will rest in hope.

Psalms 16:9

No holiday leave or even the most expensive vacation can compare to the Sabbath-rest we find in the Lord. The assurance that His presence will restore our joy and strength is guaranteed. The most difficult aspect of entering the Lord's rest, just as it is to go on holiday, is getting there.

Thank God for His rest.

Virtual Communications

You shall love the Lord your God with all your heart,
with all your soul, and with all your strength.

Deuteronomy 6:5

Not many years ago, e-mails were considered a potential phenomenon of the future. During Desert Storm, Vietnam, Korea, WWI and WWII, communication was slow and sometimes non-existent. Troops and their families simply wanted to express their love and support during deployments. Your Father doesn't need the internet to stay in touch with you—to give you the love and support you need.

With all your communicating, don't forget to tune in to God.

"What I would like to believe is that God is in this war, not as a spectator, but backing up everything that is good in us. He won't work any miracles for us because that would be helping us to do the work He's given us to do on our own. I don't know whether God goes forth with armies but I do know that He is in lots of our men or they would not do what they do."

Pvt. Walter T. Bromwich, *Company A 6th US—Engineers, American Expeditionary Forces, WWI, in a letter to his pastor in Pennsylvania.*

Sentinel Of The Soul

*No one can come to Me unless the Father
who sent Me draws him…*

John 6:44

Need proof that God wants you? It lives inside of you and
speaks to you even now. What caused you to want to read
this devotional? What moved you to talk to God? Where
did you get the longing to know God at all? Your heavenly
Father put it there. He enjoys your company and wants
you to enjoy His.

Father, thank You for my desire to come to You.

Big Little Things

He who is faithful in what is least is faithful also in much; and he who is unjust in what is least is unjust also in much.

Luke 16:10

Everyday tasks can be taxing! But it is the accomplishing of those "menial" tasks that builds the character and hones the habits fit for the great things ahead. Let me encourage you not to "stop at the half way spot." Finish the task, no matter how small. It all counts with God.

Father, help me realize that the great and the grand are not always the same thing.

The Greatness Of One

And whatever you do, do it heartily, as to the Lord and not to men, knowing that from the Lord you will receive the reward of the inheritance; for you serve the Lord Christ.

Colossians 3:23, 24

Sometimes the audience that views what we do consists not in the greatness of numbers, but the greatness of One, hallowed by the name of the Lord!

Lord, help me to do my duty today as if I am doing it just for You.

Refuge At Home

... But the Lord will be a shelter for His people, And the strength of the children of Israel.

Joel 3:16

Refuge, respite, perhaps even retirement are all made possible after loved ones are home. Prior to this moment, minds are focused on the task at hand and the uncertain future. The Lord becomes our resting place, granting to us what can only be obtained in His presence.

The Lord is my refuge and strength!

If any of you lacks wisdom, let him ask of God, who gives to all liberally and without reproach, and it will be given to him.

James 1:5

Making the decision to be a part of the military is a decision often made after much discussion. It is more than encouraging to know that the decisions made leading up to the returning home of troops are made based upon input from numerous sources.

Lord, as we welcome our troops home, give them the divine direction and connections they need to step into their future.

DATE

Over And Over

What is man that You are mindful of him, And the son of man that You visit him?

Psalms 8:4

When we think of how great and awesome God is, we are amazed at what He has done through the years in an attempt to maintain an ongoing spiritual relationship with us. By comparison, we have little, if anything to offer. Yet over and over again, He blesses us beyond our wildest imagination, simply because He loves us.

94

September 21, 1944, WWII.

Evelyn Giniger to her sweetheart Sgt. Nathan Hoffman,

"I don't know how long you'll be gone—and I don't even know if you'll want me when you come back. I think about you often, Nat—and when I heard there was a letter from you I rushed home and devoured it! And after I read it, I said to myself, "I love you, Nat." I want more than anything right now to fall completely in love with you. I hope I'm not pinning you down to anything you don't want to say, Nat—and I hope that either way everything will turn out for the best.

December 31, 1945, WWII.

Sgt. Hoffman's reply to his fiancé, Evelyn.

"For the past six weeks we've had rumor and counter-rumor of going home... This is the last day of the last month of the year, and this should be the last letter that I shall write to you. So long, honey, and pucker up—'cause here I come."

Evelyn and Nat Hoffman were married less than two months after his return from WWII.

Hope In A Box!

Let us hold fast the confession of our hope without wavering, for He who promised is faithful.

Hebrews 10:23

As I watched the Blue Star Mothers packing boxes for soldiers, I was surprised at how the contents had changed over the years. There were batteries, CD players, CD's, 35 mm cameras, and Kool Aid. The atmosphere was jovial and some of it surely found its way into the boxes. How did these mothers do it? Putting aside the bad thoughts, they tapped into the thoughts of God.

Lord, give me thoughts of peace and not of evil.

DATE

"If we confess our sins, He is faithful and just to forgive us our sins and cleanse us from all unrighteousness."

I John 1:9

Unlike children, we often feel we can make our guilt go away by trying to cover our pain with things we love. Yet, sometimes it is best to look into the eyes of God and say, "I did it." There we will find the forgiveness, the acceptance, and the love that can place healing balm on the wounds of our transgression.

Lord, I have tried to cover my pain in so many ways and nothing seems to work. So now I bring my pain and my sin to You to ask for Your forgiveness and the healing that comes from the death of Christ, my Savior.

Practice And Prayer

... these have no root...

Luke 8:13

Ever thought how easy it would be to pluck up a plant with no root? Without roots, they yield to the slightest pull. The truths of God need to take root in our lives so they are not easily taken. Prayer and practice make it happen. Decide not to be just a hearer only, but a doer.

Lord, let Your roots grow deep in me!

Stability: *Stay-bility*

Those who trust in the Lord Are like Mount Zion,
which cannot be moved, but abides forever.

Psalms 125:1

Instability is a characteristic that injects itself into people's lives. Every decision we make is potentially destabilizing. But, if we are relentless in our trust toward God, the outcome will be "stay-bility" (stability)—the ability to stay strong and courageous.

With Him at your side, you will not falter, you will not fail.

Letter from two World War II mail-deprived ensigns to a girl they've never met, but would like to:

This is a fan letter! Before I begin, let me explain that we are two very lonely lads and our morale is very low. We have hearts of gold but girls never seem to bother finding it out after once looking at our comical faces... My executive officer's name is Bill... As for looks—well he doesn't really have any. For ears, he has sort of curly protuberances that look not unlike cauliflowers. He claims he was born with them that way, but I don't believe it. God couldn't make a man with ears like that. I don't think he has any eyes, at least I've never been able to find them. He says he can see so that settles it—he has eyes. His nose looks like a large, very red apple. It is his best feature. His mouth is really a good looking one except that he has no lips. We are at a loss to explain why, he just has no lips... He claims he had a girl once, but I doubt it. Anyway, every day he wishes he would get a letter from a girl but he never does. Couldn't you surprise him with one? Girls don't like me either, but I really am a swell guy. I am not good looking, but I think I have sort of an inner beauty radiating from my heart within. I cannot explain why others don't discover it. To begin with, I have beautiful red eyes (at least you can see mine). I have a long, finely formed nose. I have the best looking ears. They are real big and they sort of stick out but attractively. I think my lips are a little thin, but you wouldn't notice them if I didn't lisp. My name is Nye, and I never had a girl in my life. Won't you write us a letter...? Bubbling over with unwanted love,

Elizabeth Jane did respond to them, but she was in love with someone else. Bill eventually returned from war. Nye did not.

DATE

"Blessed is the man who trusts in the Lord, And whose hope is the Lord."

Jeremiah 17:7

America is such a fast-paced, instant, and on-demand society. It's a challenging concept to consider the value and virtue of patience. This is a time to give over to the Lord your complete trust, knowing that He is your hope for today and tomorrow. Reorientation to the home front is a gradual process, but the Lord is not slack concerning His promises toward you this day.

Trust that the Lord knows what He is doing.

The Art Of Care Casting

… casting all your care upon Him, for He cares for you.

I Peter 5:7

Dan's father was surprised to see his son bright eyed and smiling after having spent thirteen months in the war-torn country of Afghanistan. When asked to explain, Dan answered, "When I left, I carried my burdens in my backpack. After several months, I found I carried them in my heart. When I found the Lord, it wasn't a far trip from my heart to His backpack."

Designed For Destiny

*I will praise You, for I am fearfully and wonderfully
made; Marvelous are Your works, And
that my soul knows very well.*

Psalms 139:14

Let no one degrade the wonderful soul within you. It was
made in God's image and can be transformed into something of great value.

*Lord, let not my failures nor anyone else's keep me from
knowing how You have designed, and are continuing to
design my life to have value and worth to You.*

Prejudice Deters Progress

Do not forget to entertain strangers, for by so doing some have unwittingly entertained angels.

Hebrews 13:2

When we listen to our prejudice, we may miss some of the greatest moments God has in store for us.

Father, all of us have our prejudices. Help me to overcome mine.

Led By Limitation

But Jesus looked at them and said to them, "With men this is impossible, but with God all things are possible."

Matthew 19:26

The limitations you accept are the only ones that will guide your life.

Lord, Help me not to place limitations on myself, nor let my prejudices allow me to place them on others. For all people can do great things who put their faith in God.

Consistency In Humility

Pride goes before destruction, And a haughty spirit before a fall.

Proverbs 16:18

It is not how we act when people notice, but what we do when no one is looking that accurately registers our character. Pride will deceive, but the truth will set us free.

Lord, teach me consistency. Help me be the same person whether alone or in a crowd. Forgive me when I have trusted in my own strength and with Your words of grace, show me the new person You have created in me.

DATE

*God is our refuge and strength,
A very present help in trouble.*

Psalms 46:1

Have you ever been at a loss for words with nowhere to turn for help in the time of need? It's easy for someone to tell you "don't worry, everything will work out fine." Rest assured that the Almighty is with you, from the brightest morning to the darkest night. During good times or times of trouble, He is as close as your next thought.

Trouble attracts God's presence!

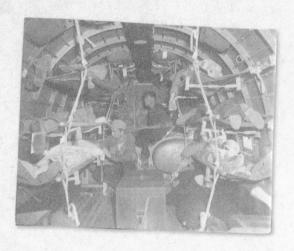

"My squadron, the 'Purple Foxes' is still over there and probably will not be back for awhile... I am retiring after 20 years of active service. Thank you so much for your prayers and support. I have no doubt that God has been watching over me and my unit, especially during Operation Iraqi Freedom."

Gunnery Sgt. Douglas R. Darling, USMC, July 2004

I will give her her vineyards from there, And the Valley of Achor as a door of hope; She shall sing there, As in the days of her youth, As in the day when she came up from the land of Egypt.

Hosea 2:15

The news that one is going home is perhaps the sweetest words ever spoken. The soldier's heart is full of joy, yet full of concern for those comrades left behind to continue the work at hand. Receptive family and friends are singing God's praise in knowing loved ones are on their way.

Lord, let me know that no praise is higher than Yours, for my Father in heaven is the true Father of us all.

The Healer With A Heart

"Judge not, and you shall not be judged. Condemn not, and you shall not be condemned. Forgive, and you will be forgiven."

Luke 6:37

It is easy to judge people quickly and superficially. It is harder to try to understand.

Lord, help me to be able to feel someone else's struggles before I so quickly judge their actions.

*You shall not take vengeance, nor bear any grudge
against the children of your people, but you shall love
your neighbor as yourself: I am the Lord.*

Leviticus 19:18

Try to remember that the final sentence doesn't come after
a man has lowered the gavel, but after God has lowered His.

*Lord, help me not to look to man and his system for justice.
Keep me ever mindful that true justice, as true grace, lies
only in Your grasp. I trust the power of Your truth.*

Be Still And Know

… the Lord passed by… but the Lord was not in the wind; … the Lord was not in the earthquake; … the Lord was not in the fire; and after the fire a still small voice.

I Kings 19:11, 12

The still small voice of God is greater than the noise of chaos, confusion, and fear. By just a word, He has the power to introduce order, compassion, and even justice. His voice of Truth is a comfort to those in trouble and a reassurance to those who worry about loved ones. It says: "I am here for you, and for them—in bright places and dark, at all times—and they can hear My voice."

Lord, speak to my heart. Calm every doubt and fear.

At The End Of Your Rope?

"Blessed are the poor in spirit, For theirs is the kingdom of heaven."

Matthew 5:3

How many times in life have you been at the end of your rope? How many times have you been at wits end? Perhaps too many times to recall. However, it was at those times that you were near to the Almighty and His rule for your life!

At the end of your Rope? God is near!

The Jesus Mindset

Let each of you look out not only for his own interests, but also for the interests of others. Let this mind be in you which was also in Christ Jesus...

Philippians 2:4, 5

Sometimes, when personal problems seem to overwhelm us, we find the solution by becoming involved with the hurts of others.

Lord, I do have my own struggles and I thank You that Your concern for my good is greater than my own. Help me empty my hands by placing my problems in Your hands. For only then can mine be free to help others.

"What a marvelous feeling to be back in this glorious country of ours. I am still awed every morning when I wake up and I can look out over the plush countryside with its green grass, rolling forested hills and blue skies overhead. It seems like I've been thru some sort of nightmare, but dawn has come and the bad dream has vanished with the coming of a new day."

Tom McCabe *in a letter to his parents written while recuperating from a Vietnam War injury in a hospital in Fort Knox, Kentucky.*

Touching God's Heart

"Take My yoke upon you and learn from Me, for I am gentle and lowly in heart, and you will find rest for your souls. For My yoke is easy and My burden is light."

Matthew 11:29, 30

He who spends his life lifting the burdens of others becomes an extension of the Master.

Lord, help me remember that when I do something to lift the load others carry, I have touched the heart of God.

National Heroes

Sing to the Lord, For He has done excellent things;
This is known in all the earth.

Isaiah 12:5

Because of national security, American families of returning soldiers must wait for loved ones to be spotted in the distance. For the soldier, it's one of the longest walks they have ever taken in their lives. The celebration is about to begin, the songs are about to ring out, the whole world is about to know that our loved ones are home.

Look what the Lord has done!

Love Makes Small Things Great

*Now he who plants and he who waters are one,
and each one will receive his own reward
according to his own labor.*

I Corinthians 3:8

"We cannot all do great things, but we can do small things
with great love." –Mother Theresa

*Lord, help me realize that what I do for You has great
significance. When done out of true compassion, it is
rewarded in heavenly earnings and is of no small
value to You.*

Seasoned With Salt

Let your speech always be with grace,
seasoned with salt ...

Colossians 4:6

Ever notice how salt can make even the white of an egg tasty? Used in large portions, it can be too bitter for consumption. Words of correction are like that. The main entrée of any conversation should never be salt. But gracious words, seasoned with salt, become a magnificently healthy diet!

Lord, help my words be full of Your grace and yet
challenge us all to change for the better.

Guam July 12, 2004

Here I am in the South
Pacific looking out at another
hot humid day. We're getting
ready to deploy and plan to be
in Hong Kong within a week.
It's good to get off the island
for a break and see how the
rest of the world lives and looks at Americans. Australia
really seemed to like us although the reception hasn't
been as good other places.

I'm staying busy working and watching as subs and ships
come in and out of Guam. We see Marines, Army and
other Naval groups as they move around the world.
Amazing to see how all of these men and women in the
military pass in the night… so to speak.

I'm really looking forward to coming home in August. I
know others who don't have families waiting for them and
it's great to have someone love and pray for me. Those
prayers truly get me through the day. Tell everyone hello
and remind them that I'm coming home soon.

Love, your son,
Tim

*Letter from **Timothy Shepherd**, US Navy*

Without Hopelessness

Do not fear therefore; you are of more value than many sparrows.

Matthew 10:31

"Hopelessness" is a word not found in the Bible. It is a word that belongs only to those who believe everything depends on their own efforts.

Lord, help me remember there is nothing out of Your sight or Your control.

Tempered With The Eternal

*Whereas you do not know what will happen tomorrow.
For what is your life? It is even a vapor that appears for
a little time and then vanishes away.*

James 4:14

Time can be filled or emptied with many things of our
choosing—a loud voice raised in anger, or a soft one filled
with compassion. Use it to take an "eye for an eye" and
everyone will be blind—or use it to see what can be made
better and bring light to everyone.

The Hunger For Home

… his father saw him and had compassion, and ran and fell on his neck and kissed him.

Luke 15:20

He was missing, he was in dire straits, and he wanted to come home. The wayward son had been gone for a long time. He had seen the good and the bad. He had felt the thrill of freedom, the power of self-will, and now the longing to be home. Going home wasn't an easy thing to do. His family might not understand the changes in the heart of this man. But still his Father's voice was crying out:

Bring him home! Bring him home! Bring him home!

Undeniable Blessings

*"Give, and it will be given to you: good measure, pressed
down, shaken together, and running over will be put into
your bosom. For with the same measure that you use, it
will be measured back to you."*

Luke 6:38

Whatever you do in life for others, the Master is aware of
and will remember in your time of need. The blessings He
bestows may come in unexpected ways, but if you wait,
never doubting, they will come—pressed down and running
over. In due time, others will see the honor the Father has
bestowed upon you, which is undeniable.

More Than Enough

Better is a dinner of herbs where love is,
Than a fatted calf with hatred.

Proverbs 15:17

"It is the heart that makes a man rich. He is rich according
to what he is, not according to what he has."
–Henry Ward Beecher

Lord, a paycheck was never designed to make a person rich.
Nor can riches make a person wealthy. Help me recognize
the things I possess that make me a blessed person and
pass them on to those I love.

Heavenly Horse Sense

For the Son of Man has come to save that which was lost.

Matthew 18:11

Horses have an innate sense that can lead them home. One evening, finding myself lost after sundown in the pouring rain, I realized that the powerful steed supporting me knew the way to safety if I would just trust him. Letting the reigns go and giving him a slight nudge of approval, I soon found myself in the safety of my own barn. Granted we took some unexpected paths, but in the end, he took me home.

Lord, when I'm confused and alone, give me the presence of mind to give You the reigns.

He did not waver at the promise of God through unbelief, but was strengthened in faith, giving glory to God...

Romans 4:20

Mere belief alone will not make us followers of Him whose Holy purpose was to prove the power of love over hate, of good over evil, of life over death. We must strive for that higher faith that comes from a dedication to become better and holier—renewed daily until it expands into a force for good that nothing can overcome.

Lord, let the affirmation of my faith, as repeated through my actions, rise into a cadence of resolve that all can march to.

One Way But No Dead Ends

Trust in the Lord with all your heart, And lean not on your own understanding; In all your ways acknowledge Him, And He shall direct your paths.

Proverbs 3:5, 6

Decisions may not be reversible but they are always fixable in God's world.

Father, let me not be wise in my own eyes, but learn to be led by You day by day.

Walking In His Way

I have taught you in the way of wisdom;
I have led you in right paths.

Proverbs 4:11

In a place of unfamiliarity and apprehension, we may believe we have wandered away from God's care. But we have His promise. If He leads us, He will provide for us. If we are lost, He will show us the way. Wherever you are, you are a choice away from finding the path to God's abundant life.

Lord, keep me in Your way.

129

Gaining Our Mind

For "who has known the mind of the Lord that he may instruct Him?" But we have the mind of Christ.

I Corinthians 2:16

Traumatic events have a way of carving great chasms into our heart and filling them with memories we would prefer to leave hidden away. They seem to come back in the middle... in the middle of the night, in the middle of a celebration, or in the middle of nothing in particular. God promises to give you the "mind of Christ." Given time, He can build a bridge from the negative to the positive.

All things will work together for good for those who love God.

*Now Hannah spoke in her heart; only her lips moved,
but her voice was not heard …*

I Samuel 1:13

As she stood there admiring her son in his full dress uni-
form, her face beamed as if her skin were translucent and
she had used a sunbeam for a smile. He was home and she
could not hide the joy. I remember the day she put him on
the bus for Ft. Hood. Her countenance was different then.
When I asked how she prayed, she said, "Sometimes there
were no words, so God and I just spoke heart to heart."

*Lord, when my words aren't right, or I find no words,
listen to my heart.*

131

If I Can Dream ...

Where there is no revelation, the people cast off restraint; But happy is he who keeps the law.

Proverbs 29:18

The poorest of all men is not the man without a cent, but the man without a dream.

Lord, help me not to live for the praise that flows from human lips but for the voice of Jesus that simply says, "Well done, thy good and faithful servant."

132

*We know that we have passed from death to life,
because we love the brethren. He who does not
love his brother abides in death.*

I John 3:14

The most important thing in life is not the triumph but the
struggle. The essential thing is not to have conquered, but
to have fought well.

*Lord, in my effort to do my best, allow me to love—for in that
is life. Let me not become so attuned to the task that I miss
Your treasure in people. Let me live and not just be alive.*

Cadences

BLUE SEAL DOG

Well I've got a dog and his name is blue.
And blue wants to be a SEAL too...
So I bought him a mask and four little fins.
I took him too the ocean and I threw his butt in.
Blue came back too my suprise.
With a shark in his teeth and gleam in his eyes.

IRAQI BLUES

Send the troops before it's too late,
Saddam has invaded Kuwait
Grab your rifle and get a tan
You can scratch a rotation plan!
1-2-3 and 4
Sometimes to get peace
ya' gotta make some war.

GONNA RUN, RUN, RUN

Up in the Morning with the Rising Sun
We're gonna run, run, run till the run is done!
What we gonna do when we get back?
Take a hot shower and hit the rack!
C-130 rolling down the strip
My fine unit is gonna take a trip.

Coming
HOME

Cadences

1775

> Back in 1775,
> My Marine Corps came alive.
> First there came the color blue,
> to show the world that we are true.
> Next there came the color red,
> to show the world the blood we shed.
> Finally there came the color green
> to show the world that we are mean.

MARINE CORP CADENCE

> I love working for Uncle Sam,
> Let's me know just who I am.
>
> 1 – 2 – 3 – 4
> United States Marine Corps!
>
> 1 – 2 – 3 – 4
> I love the Marine Corps!
>
> My Corps!
> Your Corps!
> Our Corps!
> Marine Corps!

Cadences

THE SURPRISE JUMP

Late last night, it was drizzling rain,
Lying in bed I was feeling no pain.
I heard a ringing in my head,
It was the telephone, so I jumped from my bed.
I tripped, stumbled, and said hello,
My first sergeant said it was time to go.
I got to the company, hungry as could be,
The platoon sergeant gave me an "MRE".
Chute on my back, destination unknown,
C-130 it began to groan.
Jumpmaster said now don't you know,
Stand up trooper, it's time to go.
Stand up, hook up, shuffle to the door,
Jump right out and count to four.
As I floated to the ground,
I began to look around.
Lights were shining up at me,
Where, oh, where could I be?
Jumpmaster, he had missed his spot,
This LZ was mighty hot.
Shake, fries and a "Big Mac" to go,
We landed at McDonalds, don't cha know.

Cadences

HONEY, HONEY, COMIN' HOME

I talked to my honey back home today
She's cutting the grass, throwing the trash away
Packing me a box - gonna send it soon
Filled with love - make it here by noon
Told her get ready it won't be long
We'll dance together to our favorite song

Coming
HOME

Heartfelt Thoughts

Sometimes in the whirlwind of saying goodbye to our loved ones, its easy to be overcome with so many emotions of hope, fear, anxiety, and love, that you can find no words… and all you can do is pray for a safe return, share an embrace, and shed a few tears. Here is an opportunity to write down all the things you felt, but didn't or couldn't say. Share your heartfelt thoughts and let your loved ones know how much they truly mean to you. Below are a few suggestions to help you convey your thoughts. May those who serve and those who wait be comforted as you look forward to being reunited.

When we said goodbye, I wanted to tell you…

These are my hopes for you…

Coming
HOME

I want you to know…

_____

_____

_____

_____

_____

_____

_____

I am reminded of you when…

_____

_____

_____

_____

_____

_____

_____

Coming
HOME

OFFICIAL U. S. MARINE CORPS PHOTO
By Staff Sgt. M. A. Cornelius

OUT BUT NOT DOWN

This Fifth Division marine was fighting in the front lines of Iwo Jima when a Jap mortar shell landed beside him. Badly shaken but still on his feet, he was hurried to the rear by two supporting comrades.

Are you buying War Bonds to hurry their return home?

NORRIS BROS. Inc.

DAN NORRIS   PAUL NORRIS

Coming
HOME

For Those Who Serve and Those Who Wait.